£5.95

1997

Residential Care
Options for Later Life

AGE
CONCERN
SCOTLAND

Edinburgh: The Stationery Office Limited

Residential Care
Options for Later Life

The Stationery Office Limited
South Gyle Crescent, Edinburgh EH12 9EB

Applications for reproduction should be made to The Stationery Office Limited

First published 1997

British Library Cataloguing in Publication Data

A catalogue record for this book is available from the British Library

ISBN 0 11 495839 4

Cover illustration by Steve Earl

Contents

About Age Concern

Age Concern Scotland is committed to working throughout Scotland to ensure that all older people:

- have their rights upheld
- have their needs addressed
- have their voices heard
- have choice and control over all aspects of their lives.

Age Concern Scotland:

- supports a network of groups across Scotland providing support and services to older people
- campaigns on issues affecting older people
- aims to influence policy and practice in the care of older people.

Age Concern Scotland works closely with Age Concern centres in England, Wales and Northern Ireland to form a network of over 1,400 independent local UK groups. These groups, with the invaluable help of an estimated 250,000 volunteers, aim to improve the quality of life for older people and develop services appropriate to local needs and resources. These include day care, visiting services, transport schemes, advice and information, clubs and specialist facilities for disabled older people.

About the Author

Rosemary Bland is a lecturer in Social Work at the University of Stirling. She is currently on secondment to the Scottish Office Social Work Services Inspectorate as an inspector. She is the editor of *Developing Services for Older People and their Families* and the co-author of *Residential Homes for Elderly People: Their Cost and Quality*. The views expressed in this book are those of the author and do not represent inspectorate or government policy.

Acknowledgements

I would like to thank the following people for their comments on the text: Lucie McKenzie and Sue Ramsden, Age Concern Scotland; Evelyn McEwan, Age Concern England; Robert Taylor, Age Concern Wales; and Penny Fleming, Edinburgh and Leith Age Concern.

Introduction

Older people tend to consider residential care when they feel that they, or those who look after them, can no longer manage as things stand. Perhaps you or a close relative or friend are in this position. If so, you need information about the options, and about life in residential and nursing homes.

Since the first edition of this book, *Residental Care: Is It for Me?*, was published in 1987, there have been many changes in the way that care and support for older people are organised. There are now more options available to those who need support in managing their daily lives. Some of these options may help people avoid having to move house – a stressful event at any age. This means that you should have more choices available when deciding what to do.

This book starts by looking at the reasons why an older person, or the relative or adviser of an older person, may wish to find out about the options and choices available. It then considers all sorts of services which help older people to stay in their own homes yet still get the support they need. The second part of the book looks at the various types of residential and nursing home care available. Several new models of residential care have been developed in the last 10 years and we look at how these differ from the more traditional residential home. The final part explains what financial help is available to older people. It also explains the charges for residential and nursing home care and how you can get help with these costs.

Thinking about making major changes in your life is difficult and can be unsettling. The aim of this book is to give you ideas and information about the help available if you are finding it difficult to manage at home and are thinking that you might have to move. If you are a relative or adviser helping an older person to make plans, this book will give you a range of useful information. It is written in the form of questions and answers. The questions asked reflect my experience of talking with older people and are amongst those frequently asked of Age Concern organisations.

Sometimes older people have to make a decision about residential care in a hurry because of illness or as a result of an accident. If at all possible, take time to consider your options. I hope this book helps you to make the right decision for you.

Rosemary Bland

Part 1
Should I Move?

Part 1

Should I Move?

In this part we look at the reasons why you may be thinking about getting more help, either in your own home or by moving into a residential care home or nursing home.

Why think about moving?

Whether through accident or illness or because of increasing age and disability, you may find that your present arrangements at home no longer meet your needs. If you are living alone with support and help from your family, they may be finding it more difficult to provide the help you need or you may be uncomfortable having to rely increasingly on their help. Perhaps you have been looking after someone and finding it increasingly hard to manage, or possibly your spouse or partner has died and you find it hard to continue living on your own. Getting out of the house may have become difficult or impossible and you may be feeling isolated or lonely. Or the upkeep of your home is becoming an increasing financial burden, perhaps because it is too large, requires expensive repairs or is difficult to heat.

If you feel that you need help, the first thing to do is to talk to someone. If you contact the social work or social services department of the local council, you can ask for an 'assessment' of your needs. Someone will come to see you to discuss what help you might need and tell you what is available. At the end of this book you will find a list of addresses of useful organisations and information on how to contact local sources of help (see pp. 73–78).

1

Staying at Home

If you would really rather stay at home, you will want to find out what help you can get to make this possible. The range and type of services, and whether and how much you have to pay for them, varies across the country. This chapter outlines the different types of help available, and where to go to get the help you need.

Can I get help with daily living?

If you need help with daily living you can ask someone from the social work or social services department of your local council to visit you and 'assess' or find out what your needs are. This might be done by a social worker, occupational therapist or care manager. They should also assess the needs of anyone who is helping to look after you, often referred to as a 'carer'. They will then discuss with you what sort of assistance you might need and tell you what help you might expect to get.

What about a home help?

The social work or social services department may be able to offer a home help (now usually called home care) to assist you at home. The type of tasks that they can do varies from area to area, but it *should* depend on what you need. This may be cleaning the house, meal preparation, shopping or personal care. The range of services provided by home care is now much wider than just domestic help. It can range from help to get up and dressed, to a helping you to bed and 'tucking up' service. Home care services are now more likely to be available at night and at weekends.

The home help may be able to take over some of the help your relatives or friends have previously been giving. The aim is to meet your needs in a way which is most acceptable to you and your family.

Some voluntary organisations provide home care services to older people. Local Crossroads Care Attendant Schemes give carers a break from caring by providing practical help and high quality care for people with disabilities. 'Meals on wheels' may be provided by the Women's Royal Voluntary Service or by a local Age Concern group. They can be contacted through the social work or social services department.

Home care services are also available privately, for example from companies who offer domestic help, or sometimes from other private care agencies such as private nursing or residential homes. You can find them listed in the Yellow Pages under 'domestic services'. The local social work or social services department do not have any special control over the standards offered by such agencies at present.

What equipment, aids or adaptations could make my life easier?

If you have difficulty with activities such as getting about the house, cooking a meal, or bathing, there is a wide range of aids and equipment which can help you to stay independent. There are various kinds of walking aids available, and there are adapted kitchen tools for people who have difficulty, for example, grasping objects or opening tins.

If you cannot get in and out of the bath safely, a bath seat and rails or a shower cabinet might be what you want. If the problem is that you can no longer climb the stairs, a stair lift might be the answer.

How can I find out about aids and equipment?

If you ask for help from the social work/social services department, an occupational therapist can assess your needs for all types of aids, adaptations and equipment. They should be able to help with advice and, in some cases, by supplying what you need. However, you may have to wait some time for a visit and then have a further wait before equipment can be provided or installed because budgets for equipment are limited and demand has increased.

Hospitals also have occupational therapy departments and they may be able to supply some equipment to people who have recently been patients. The Red Cross lends equipment such as wheelchairs, walking frames and commodes to people on a short term basis.

If you need a large piece of equipment such as a wheelchair on a permanent basis, this can only be provided free of charge if it is requested by your GP who will refer you to a health service rehabilitation or aid centre. Electric wheelchairs which operate indoors and outdoors may be available in some circumstances.

Some large chains of chemists now have a wide selection of equipment and aids on sale to the general public, and some specialist shops sell larger items such as wheelchairs. However, these are expensive, and if you have a medical need for a wheelchair, it should be available to you through the National Health Service.

Can I get help with sight or hearing problems?

If you have a sensory disability, such as reduced hearing or sight, the Royal National Institute for the Deaf and the Royal National Institute for the Blind can supply some aids such as talking books, visible doorbells etc. You can contact them direct or ask the local authority social worker for sensory disability to visit you and make enquiries on your behalf. The local authority may also be able to loan items of equipment or refer you to a local source of help.

Can I get help to cope with incontinence?

If you are troubled by occasional or regular incontinence, your GP will be able to help. They may refer you to a physiotherapist who can teach you exercises to help you overcome or manage your problem. The community nurse at your local health centre will either put you in touch with a specialist continence adviser or tell you about products which can help you manage the problem successfully. The local district nursing service may be able to help you with supplies of continence promoting aids and equipment. A commode near the bed may help and this may be supplied by an occupational therapist or community nurse or may be loaned by your local branch of the Red Cross. You can also buy your own commode.

Where can I get more information on equipment?

Disabled Living Centres throughout the country have equipment on permanent display which people with disabilities can try out. Disabled Living Centres vary in size and type, and may be run by voluntary organisations, health authorities or local authority social work or social service departments.

If you live in England or Wales, the Disabled Living Foundation is a good point of contact. If you live in Scotland, Disability Scotland will be able to advise you. See the useful addresses at the end of the book (p. 73).

If you need major adaptations to your home and you are a council tenant your local authority housing department may be able to carry these out. If you own your home, you may be eligible for a grant from your local authority. Getting these adaptations approved and carried out can take several months.

What help can I get to keep my home warm?

Energy Advice Centres can advise on all types of heating problems and on home insulation. They can help you to claim grants for draught-proofing and insulation and advise on more efficient ways of heating your home. The address of your local centre will be in the telephone directory. Information on grants is also available from the Energy Action Grants Agency (see useful addresses, p. 73)

Can I get any help with house repairs?

Many people find the prospect of getting quotations and dealing with tradespeople and suppliers quite daunting.

Many parts of the country now have 'Care and Repair' or 'Staying Put' schemes which assist older people with all the aspects of getting alterations carried out to their home. This can include help with making planning applications (where these are necessary), advice on grants available, getting help with paying for the cost of the improvement/alteration, getting quotations and supervising the work. They may also arrange temporary alternative accommodation if you have to move out while the work is being done.

'Care and Repair' or 'Staying Put' projects may be run by your local council, Age Concern, or local housing associations. The housing department of your local council or the Citizens' Advice Bureau should be able to tell you if there is such a scheme in your area. These schemes can only help home owners and tenants of private landlords. If you are a council or housing association tenant your landlord has the responsibility for carrying out the repairs to your home.

Can I get an emergency alarm system?

If you wish to remain in your own home but are worried about having an accident and not being able to summon help, you may find it reassuring to have an alarm system installed. These can be bought privately, rented through housing associations or can be provided through local authority housing or social work or social services departments. The agency which is responsible for alarm schemes varies across the country, so you will need to enquire locally. There may be several schemes in your area, allowing you some choice of system.

There are two main kinds of alarm system: one is linked to the telephone and the other relies on pressure pads.

Some telephone linked alarms have a pendant which you wear around your neck or on your wrist. In an emergency, you only have to press the pendant and the control centre will be alerted. Some alarm schemes enable you to speak to the scheme co-ordinator and say what is wrong. Others automatically relay the call for help to a member of staff from the scheme, or dial the number of one of a previously agreed list of people, when the alarm is activated.

Pressure pad alarms are placed under your doormat or in your toilet. They activate a centrally controlled alarm system if the toilet is not flushed or if no one crosses the doormat of your house within a certain period of time.

What help can I get outside the house?

You may be interested in attending a local lunch club or day centre. These are run by local authority social work or social services departments or by voluntary organisations, such as Age Concern. They may be in church or community halls, sheltered housing lounges or sometimes in units of residential homes. They may provide transport to and from the centre, meals, company, entertainment, activities and outings. Some schemes are able to offer a range of services: these can include assistance with a bath, laundry, hairdressing, chiropody and welfare benefits advice.

Your local authority social work or social services department should be able to give details of all day services for older people in your area.

What help is there for people with dementia?

Some local authorities and voluntary organisations provide services particularly for people who have one of a range of illnesses called dementia, the most common of which is Alzheimer's Disease.

Some day care groups are happy to have a proportion of people with dementia attending; others cater solely for people with dementia. Some schemes welcome family carers who wish to remain with their relative. Familiar surroundings, a calm atmosphere, good lighting and clear signs can make a big difference to how a person with dementia feels in a new place and how well they can adapt and find their way around.

A range of support services and new sorts of residential care are now being developed for people with dementia. You will be able to find out what services exist in your area for people with dementia and for their family and carers through your GP, community psychiatric nurse or social work or social services department.

What help is available for carers?

Carers are now entitled to have their own needs assessed, as well as the needs of the person they are caring for.

Crossroads Care Attendant schemes specialise in providing services to relieve the pressure on people caring at home for someone with a disability. Schemes vary in what they can provide up and down the country so you should enquire locally. Not all areas have Crossroads Schemes.

Alzheimer's groups and some social work or social services departments run carers' groups. Many people find such a group helps to overcome the sense of isolation which some people caring on their own can feel. These schemes usually have some link with a 'sitting' service which can enable the person caring to attend the group while someone stays with their relative. See Useful Addresses (p. 73) at the end of the book for organisations which provide support for carers.

The range of help available to support you if you wish to carry on living in your own home varies from area to area. If you have a disability you may also be entitled to extra financial help (see Part 3). If you do continue to live in your own home you may occasionally need extra care or help for a short period and the following chapter looks at the different kinds of help available.

2

Short Breaks

This chapter describes how you, or your carer can get help for a short break, for example when your family goes on holiday.

Can I get a short break?

Short breaks, sometimes called 'respite care' can provide a break for someone who needs care, whether they live on their own or with others. Some local authority and residential homes run by voluntary organisations may have special units or bedrooms which are set aside for people who want to come for a short stay. Residential homes run by private organisations, and sometimes nursing homes, may offer short stay opportunities, but usually only when they have long stay beds vacant.

Short stays may also be used for a 'trial' stay to see if you would like to move in permanently, and to see if the home can provide the level of care that you need.

How can I arrange 'respite' care?

If the local authority agrees that you need a period of 'respite care' then you may be entitled to help with the cost from your local authority (see Part 3, p. 61). If you wish to make the arrangements and pay for yourself then you can do so, though you may wish to contact the local authority for advice.

If you or your family are trying to plan ahead for a specific period, say for a holiday, you are most likely to be able to make a secure booking in a local authority home. The local authority may have a contract with a private or voluntary home to provide a number of short stay beds. You, or a relative, will need to contact your local social work or social services office.

If you have special needs, it is important to check which homes can cater for these. Be sure to mention, for example, if you are unable to climb stairs or if you use a wheelchair, if you have sight, speech or hearing difficulties or if you have special dietary, religious or cultural needs.

If the aim is to have a 'trial stay' to see whether you like the home enough to take up long term residence, make this clear.

Rehabilitative short stays

If your physical or mental health is poor, a few weeks stay in a residential or nursing home might be beneficial. Your GP may support your request by writing to the local social work/social services department, who will arrange this if they agree this is what you need. If you are very frail and have special needs, then a 'respite' or short stay in hospital may be more appropriate. This can be arranged by your GP.

Sometimes you may benefit from a period of attendance at a day hospital in order to receive services such as physiotherapy, speech therapy or occupational therapy. This would have to be requested by and through your GP. A hospital doctor specialising in the treatment of older people – a geriatrician or psychogeriatrician – may visit you at home first to see what help or treatment you need or you may be asked to attend an out-patient clinic at your local day hospital.

Home-based schemes

In some areas, local authorities have set up respite or Home Break schemes which recruit people to take an older or disabled person into their own home for a short break. People in the scheme are carefully recruited by the local authority social work or social services department. They will usually be given training in aspects of caring and may have a nursing or residential care background or may have cared for parents or family members in the past.

People using these schemes are matched with the 'carers' to try and ensure compatibility. These schemes can be very successful and may provide an opportunity for a break several times a year.

Getting help in your own home

You may not want to have to go away to get help or care when you need it. This may be particularly true if the care is only needed for a week or two, perhaps while the carer goes away for a holiday. There are schemes run by voluntary organisations (such as Crossroads Care Attendant schemes) which can provide someone to move into your home. Some local authorities are trying out such schemes, in some cases jointly with the local health authority. Private nursing and home care agencies may also offer this type of service. One way to assure the quality of the service is to check that the agency belongs to a national association which sets standards for its members.

These chapters have looked at what help and support is available to enable you to live in your own home. The rest of the book goes on to consider the options available if you decide that you need to make a move.

Part 2
Making a Move

Part 2

Making a Move

This part considers the options available for someone who has decided that they are no longer able to remain in the same house and need to move. You may find that there is a range of different kinds of housing or accommodation with support within your area.

3

Moving to Supported Housing

If your home is too large, or if you cannot carry out alterations to make it easier to manage, you may consider a move into a sheltered house or flat. In order to qualify for the title 'sheltered housing' most schemes have to have a minimum of a resident warden or 'warden on call' system and an emergency alarm system. Some schemes may have additional facilities such as laundry rooms with washing and drying machines, communal lounges, organised activities and guest bedrooms for friends or relatives to come and stay.

Could I move to sheltered housing?

Sheltered housing is available to buy or to rent. Sheltered housing to rent is provided by local authorities or housing associations, whereas the housing which is for sale is built by private developers or housing associations. The terms and conditions which apply to such schemes vary enormously. You should find out as much as possible about those that interest you before making any decisions.

Sheltered housing schemes for people from black and minority ethnic communities are now being developed, often by local housing associations catering for particular minority ethnic groups.

What about very sheltered or care housing?

People who move into sheltered housing are usually still able to do most things for themselves. For those who already need some level of care, however, some housing associations have now developed very sheltered, care or extra care housing schemes. Accommodation in very sheltered schemes may consist of a large bed-sitting-room with its own private bath or shower-room. These schemes differ from ordinary sheltered housing in that they have staff who may provide cooked meals and assistance with getting up, dressing and showering or bathing as well as the services provided by the warden.

For people with severe memory difficulties (often due to dementia) there are some specialist schemes in which staff help tenants to retain as much control over their daily lives as possible, while being on hand to assist them when needed. Some housing associations have developed highly supportive models of care housing specially for people with dementia and are having considerable success in caring for such residents, often being able to care for them to the end of their lives.

Your local council housing department will be able to tell you what sheltered housing is available in your area.

How much does sheltered housing cost?

In addition to mortgage or rent, and council tax, there will most likely be management fees payable, covering upkeep of the grounds and the warden's salary. This may be a considerable sum in some schemes and is likely to increase every year.

There may, however, be some financial advantages to sheltered housing, such as a much reduced television licence fee and some shared heating costs. You may also be able to get help with the cost of rent and service charges through Housing Benefit (see Part 3 – Income and Finance).

Some organisations which manage owner-occupier sheltered housing schemes may take a percentage of any profit made when the property changes hands and plough it back into the scheme. If you have owned the property for a considerable time, this could amount to a substantial sum. It is important to read any scheme leaflets or brochures carefully, ask about anything you are unsure of, and get independent advice before making any commitment.

4

Moving to a Residential Home

This chapter looks at choosing a residential care home and what life might be like after you have moved in.

First steps

It can be a very difficult decision to move into a care home but there are many homes where the quality of care is excellent and in which people can lead full lives. Some residential care homes are run by local authorities, and some by the private sector or by voluntary and religious organisations. Homes vary a great deal in size, cost, atmosphere and in terms of the facilities they offer. Unlike nursing homes, a residential care home does not necessarily have a qualified nurse as part of the staff.

The process of moving into a residential care home depends on who is meeting the cost. If you are able to pay for the care from your own financial resources, the local authority need not be involved at all and you can make your enquiries and visit any homes which interest you before deciding whether or not to go ahead and make the move.

The registration section of your local authority social work or social services department can provide you with a list of all registered homes in the area. You can ask the local authority inspection unit to let you see their reports on homes you are interested in, but the amount of information in these reports varies widely. However, you may wish to contact your local authority for advice before making private residential care arrangements. This is to ensure that you are aware of all the available options, and in case you need financial help in the future.

If you want help with the cost of residential care, you *must* ask the social work or social services department of the local council to assess your need for care. They can only help with the cost of residential care home fees if they agree that you need this type of care (see Part 3 – Paying for Care).

If they think that there are other ways of meeting your needs, they will tell you what services can be provided, whilst offering you as much choice as possible. Alternative ways of supporting you at home may include home help, meals on wheels, a help call or alarm system and maybe a place at a day care centre. An occupational therapist may be asked to look at your home and your difficulties and suggest what aids or adaptations could make life easier and more manageable for you (see Part 1 – Staying at Home).

What happens when I am 'assessed'?

This is the process whereby the social worker (or care manager, as s/he may be called) visits you to decide how your needs can best be met. The visit will consist of an interview in which you will be asked about your difficulties and how you have managed life up to now. Your views about your situation and your wishes regarding the possible solutions to your difficulties will be taken into account.

If there are any points you are uncertain about, or if there is anything which is not clear to you, do say so and ask for an explanation. Ask for any written information available, so that you can go over it after the visit and check up on any points you may have overlooked or misunderstood. There will be a form to complete which you will probably be asked to sign as a way of confirming that you know what information has been recorded. You should receive a copy of the written assessment. After the assessment a written 'care plan' should be drawn up with you. You should be given a copy of this.

Your GP will be asked to provide information about your physical and mental health. You may also be asked to agree to an examination by a geriatrician or psychogeriatrician as part of the overall assessment of your needs. Some homes which are run by religious organisations may require a reference from your minister or religious leader before considering or confirming an application.

Can I have a trial stay?

If you are uncertain whether you would settle happily into a residential care home, ask if you can stay for a weekend or an overnight stay. Whether the home can grant such a request will probably depend on whether it has vacancies when you make contact. You may wish to move in on a trial basis for a period of say, a month. A trial stay can be helpful for both you and the staff in coming to a decision about whether this is the right place for you.

Can I get written information about the home?

Most homes should have a brochure or information leaflet of some kind. They should also offer some form of written contract, which sets out essential information such as the kind of accommodation you are being offered and the charges you are being asked to pay. This will include what services the charges cover as well as the amount of notice you or they are required to give if you leave.

How much choice will I have if I am getting help to pay the fees?

If the social worker's (or care manager's) assessment is that your needs can best be met in a residential care home, they should offer you a choice of homes in the area you wish to live. These may be run by the local authority or by a voluntary or private organisation. The local authority will have a list of registered homes whose charges are within a range that it is prepared to meet. You should be given written information about these homes. If you prefer a more expensive home and someone else can pay the extra fee, this is also possible.

You should take the opportunity to visit the homes which currently have vacancies (or get a relative, friend or adviser to visit if you are unable to go yourself). It is very useful to see what they are like, and what facilities they offer.

Can I keep my home on for a while?

Once the decision is made about which home you are moving into and when, you can make plans regarding your own home. If your home is rented you may not have to give up your tenancy straight away. Tenants going into residential care can continue to receive Housing Benefit to cover their rent for up 13 weeks while they are settling into long term accommodation, as long as the stay is for a trial period.

If you own your home and no one else lives in it, and you are not going to be able to meet the residential home fees from your savings or income, you may have to sell your home (see Part 3 – Paying for Care).

Can I complain about the assessment of what care I need?

If you disagree with or are unhappy about the assessment, then you have the right to say so. Local authority social work or social service departments must provide a complaints procedure for anyone who disagrees with the assessment or is unhappy about it. The person who assesses you should tell you about the procedure for making complaints.

Reviewing your decision to move in

The home may have a formal process for reviewing with you whether you have settled happily and wish to make the arrangement permanent. Local authority homes and some run by voluntary organisations will have a process they call a 'review' to confirm with the home and yourself that the arrangement is satisfactory to all parties. Once this review is completed, you may get a contract or letter offering long term care. If you decide to stay there, this is the point at which to give up your tenancy or to put your house up for sale if necessary.

What happens if the home turns out not to be suitable?

If you are unhappy with the residential care home you move into, you can ask the social work or social services department to try and find you somewhere else to live. Your right to financial help will be unchanged by such a move. It will be important to be able to discuss what it was that you did not like in the first home in order to try and avoid such a feature in any future home.

Is it a home for life?

Some residential care homes are more able than others to continue to provide care for residents even when they become very frail. You may wish to avoid, if at all possible, a further move. It is worth talking to the owner or manager about their attitude to increasing disability and terminal care and whether or not they would expect you to move to a nursing home if you became very frail. You are less likely to be asked to move if the home is registered as both a residential care and nursing home.

What about couples?

Sometimes one member of a couple becomes ill or has an accident which makes them very dependent on the other person for some of their daily needs. The difficulty may be due to physical or mental illness or sometimes both. In some cases, the care needed is too great for the fitter member of the couple to provide at home and it may safeguard the health and welfare of you both if you consider moving into a residential care home together.

One of the major considerations in these circumstances is the cost, and whether you would need help in paying for care (see Part 3 – Paying for Care). If the 'fit' member of the couple can be supported at home, the local authority may not be willing to pay for both of you to go into residential care. If the 'fit' person needs care themselves or if it is important to the less fit person's mental welfare that the couple should stay together, then financial support for both may be possible.

It is more unusual for a couple to move into a residential care home than for someone on their own. Homes tend to have single beds, so if you and your partner prefer a double bed, check that you can take it in with you and that the room you are offered is large enough to accommodate it comfortably along with any other pieces of furniture you wish to take.

Can someone with dementia move into a residential care home?

Some residential care homes cater specially for people with dementia. Some homes run by local authorities may have a part of the home set aside for people with dementia. However, it is possible that a social worker assessing your needs would suggest that you need care in a nursing home. This might avoid the need to move from a residential care home if your need for care increased. One very important factor for people with dementia is continuity. It follows, then, that, if at all possible, people with dementia should not have to face more than one move after leaving their home.

What points should I consider when choosing a home?

Where do I want to live?

First of all, you need to decide whether you want to move nearer your family, if they live some distance away, or whether you want to remain in the area you know and where your friends are.

Next, think about whether the home is convenient for shops, post office, bank, library, hairdresser, place of worship, health centre or pub. Is it well situated for catching a bus, or a train or getting a taxi if local facilities are out of walking distance for you?

Do I want to live in a town or in the country?

If you have always lived in a town, you may find it easier to continue doing so. Some people love the idea of living in the country in theory. However, if there is no transport available you may become rather isolated and visitors may find it impossible or difficult to get to see you very often. Some homes which are in the country have their own transport which may overcome the risk of isolation and the advantages of the location may then outweigh any difficulties.

Do I need somewhere without stairs?

If you have difficulty or find it impossible to use stairs you may prefer to live in a home which is built all on one level because this will enable you to move about the home with greater independence. However, most private and voluntary homes are in converted former private houses and may well have stairs. There will most likely be a passenger lift or a stair lift. You may wish to see if you can use these on your own or whether you would need assistance to do so.

Do I like the look of the home?

Does the outside of the home look attractive and inviting? Is it in good condition and if there is a garden, does it look well tended? Visit the home and ask to look around it. If you are shown the public rooms, you will be able to see how much activity there is and what form it takes. If there is a television on, are people actively watching it or is it just a background noise? Find out from staff if there is any special entertainment. Ask about the activities and hobbies that particularly interest you.

What do existing residents think of the home?

Ask for a private word with one or two residents of the home, bearing in mind that nowhere will please everyone who lives there and people place greater importance on some things than others. Ask what training the staff working there have received. Caring sensitively for frail older people requires skills which have to be learned and a caring and compassionate nature may not be enough.

Does the home feel welcoming and attractive?

Are you attracted by the 'atmosphere' of the home? Is the person who is in charge someone you could have confidence in and with whom you could get on easily? How about other staff and the residents? Does the home have an informative brochure which sets out what it aims to offer people living there and gives details about what it provides? Does it give the impression that individual residents' rights are safeguarded?

The physical appearance of a residential care home and the facilities it offers are important, and so is the impression you have of it. Do the existing residents seem to enjoy being there and is the home used by residents as they wish? Living with a group of people means that total freedom to do what one wishes is impossible but some homes are much better than others at being flexible and giving their residents maximum independence and choice over how they live their lives.

What sorts of rules does the home have?

It is important not to assume anything about residential care homes as they vary enormously. Some may have no written rules or regulations but nevertheless give one the feeling that daily life is very much under staff control. Others may have a list of regulations in their brochure, for example, some homes have rules about smoking and drinking.

How life is organised in residential care homes is very much influenced by the person in charge. Even homes run by the same organisation will differ from each other, so make specific enquiries at the home you are considering.

What is the food like and how flexible are arrangements about meals?

Food is important to most people. See if there is a sample of weekly menus available and whether it is the same choice every week or whether it varies. You might like to know how much choice is available at mealtimes or whether there is only one set main dish. The whole question of special dietary needs will also be important for some people. If you are a vegetarian, or have to follow a special diet for medical or religious reasons be sure to ask whether your needs can be met.

Ask residents about quality and quantity and whether meals are available flexibly or only at specified times. Can residents have meals in their rooms if they feel like it or are they expected to take them in the dining room? Knowing in advance what homes are like will help you choose the one which is most appropriate for you.

Are single rooms available and can I get en-suite facilities?

One good piece of news about residential homes is that more and more of them are now offering single bedrooms and, increasingly, although more slowly, en-suite toilet and washing or bathing/showering facilities. If two people want to share a room, there are still plenty of homes which offer twin-bedded rooms but most people, given the choice, prefer a room to themselves. The down side of this brighter picture is that single rooms and rooms with private facilities are likely to be more expensive in private homes and also in some homes run by voluntary organisations.

Will I have to share a bedroom?

When you discuss your needs with the social worker who visits you to assess your requirements, be sure to say whether or not you are willing to share a room. Some rooms are more spacious than others and some homes better at safeguarding the privacy of people sharing a bedroom. For instance, you might wish to have a screen or curtains you could draw to give you privacy when dressing or undressing or a screen round a washhand-basin if there is one in the room. Of course, screens do not keep out sound and if you need to use a commode at night you may feel a single room is essential.

The social worker will have to balance the urgency of your need for a residential care home with the availability of suitable, affordable accommodation in the area you wish. This may be difficult at times. However, most homes do have a proportion of single rooms and if you are asked to share initially, you may be able to get a room to yourself when a vacancy occurs.

Will there be adequate toilet facilities?

If you need to use the toilet frequently, or have difficulty getting there speedily or in time, it will be especially important for you to find a home which is well supplied with easily accessible bathrooms and toilets.

What is life inside residential care homes like?

Will I still be able to see my own GP?

This depends on where you take up residence and on the attitude of your GP. Generally, GPs are happy to continue to attend a patient who moves into a residential care home if it is still within the area covered by their practice. Local authority social work/services homes consider that it is good practice to enable someone moving into a home to keep the same general practitioner, if at all possible, and they try very hard to achieve this. However, the final decision is one that is taken by your GP.

If you move away from your previous residential area you may no longer be covered by your original general practice or health centre and you will need to find a new GP. Some homes come to an arrangement with the local health centre GPs whereby everyone in the home has the same GP. This can be easier for the doctors and the home staff but is not necessarily in the best interests of the individual residents.

You may consider it useful to find out, if you do have to change to a new GP, whether the practice in the home is for you to see them at their surgery if you are able, or in private, in your own bedroom, if you are too unwell to go to them. Some homes may wish to have a member of staff present at consultations.

What will happen to any medicines I take?

When you move into a residential care home the staff will feel a measure of responsibility for your well-being. They will want to know whether you are taking any medication and what it is, in case you are suddenly taken ill. Some homes may encourage you to continue to look after your own medicines, if you are happy to do that, provided they can be safely secured in a locked drawer or cupboard in your bedroom.

Some homes have useful boxes which can allow you to put any tablets you may be taking into separate sections marked for each day of the week. This can help you to avoid making mistakes. In some homes staff may ask you to give them your medication and they will assume responsibility for giving you the necessary medicines as you need them.

Are there staff available at night if needed?

You might like to ask individual homes what arrangements they offer for people at night if they need assistance. They will have to follow the local authority guidelines which will probably lay down the requirement for waking night staff to be available in homes.

Can I furnish and decorate my own bedroom?

There is no one answer to this question because homes vary so much. It is now regarded as good practice to encourage older people moving into residential care homes to take at least some of their personal furniture and possessions with them, to help personalise their new accommodation. However, room size or design, or fixed equipment such as built-in wardrobes or wash-hand basins may limit the amount and size of furniture which you can take.

Generally, homes will encourage you to take at least some furniture and personal items in with you. Some homes are happy for residents to have their room re-decorated by a family member or at their own expense. Some local authority run homes offer residents the chance to choose their bedroom wallpaper if the home is about to be re-decorated.

Expectations about what homes should provide are rising; Jacuzzis and individual televisions are now provided in some places – generally the more expensive homes, unfortunately!

Will my possessions be secure?

If you have valuable possessions, such as jewellery, you will be expected to take out your own insurance cover for this. Some homes will provide keys to individual residents' rooms but not all will do so. Most homes will provide at least a lockable cupboard even if the bedroom door is not lockable.

What choice will I have about getting up and going to bed and taking a bath or shower?

Good practice in residential care homes emphasises the importance of giving people as many choices about their lives as possible. How much choice staff can actually give to individual residents may depend on how many of the residents need assistance from staff to get out of bed or to get dressed or undressed and how many staff are on duty at busy times of the morning and evening. Some homes give residents breakfast in bed so that people's need for help can be managed over a longer period in the morning. In the evening there should not be a problem, unless everyone wants to go to bed at the same time, which is unlikely.

Bathing can be difficult for people to do on their own unless bathrooms have been thoughtfully designed and are well equipped with aids. Most homes encourage residents to accept at least some degree of assistance from staff with bathing, even if this is no more than a hand to get safely in and out of the bath. You might want to ask what the arrangements are for bathing: can you have a bath when you want one and will the member of staff be the same sex as yourself? Some homes have showers which even very disabled people can use independently – some are designed especially for wheelchair users to manage on their own. This is the ideal, but such equipment is expensive and is not available everywhere. If you are a wheelchair user you will want to know the arrangements available in any home you are considering.

Will it be possible to do any personal laundry?

Some people like to wash out their own 'smalls' and most homes will encourage residents to continue doing so if they wish. Some homes may offer a personal laundry service (which may or may not be included in the fees). In some homes there are domestic washing machines for residents' use if they wish to launder their own clothing. Bed linen and towels are usually laundered by the home. You may wish to ask how often these are changed.

Is it possible to get services like chiropody, physiotherapy, dentistry, optical services or hairdressing in the home?

Where people are able to go out of the home to get these services, they would be encouraged to continue doing so, attending the same practitioners if at all possible and if they so wish. However, where a resident is unable to go out to the service, it may be possible to arrange for a visit to be made to the home. Medical services such as physiotherapy, speech therapy or occupational therapy will need to be requested by and through your GP, as they would in your own home. Some homes may have a private arrangement with a chiropodist or physio-therapist and these services may be available to you as part of your care or through paying an additional, optional charge.

Most local authority homes have arrangements with local dentists and optometrists who will be willing to see you in the home if you are unable to go to their premises. Likewise most homes have a visiting hairdresser for people who cannot go out to one or who wish to use the in-house service. Private and voluntary homes vary a great deal in what they offer in the way of services. Generally, the more facilities they have available, the higher the fees, rather like hotels.

Think about the services that you use at home and consider what you would need if you move into a residential care home. If they are important to you, check that you can either get out to them or that they can come to you in the home.

Will I be able to have visitors when I want?

Some homes welcome visitors at any time. However, a few, isolated recent scares about intruders have made home owners and managers more concerned about security. It may, therefore, not be as easy as it once was for visitors to 'pop in' to see residents at any time. On the whole, people are welcome during the daytime, sometimes being asked to avoid mealtimes, but not always. Sometimes visitors are welcome to join residents for a meal.

In some larger homes, there are plenty of lounges, sitting rooms and quiet corners where visitors can be received and entertained. If people have their own bedroom, they may prefer to take visitors there to talk in private. Where bedrooms are shared, this can be difficult sometimes. Some homes have tea- and coffee-making facilities especially for visitors and others may provide refreshments.

Will there be restrictions about going out or coming back into the home?

Most homes will encourage people to go out and about as much as they are able. Staff will usually ask that you tell them when you are going to be out so that meals are not wasted and they can account for you in an emergency, such as a fire. Most homes, like some hotels, shut the front door at a specific time at night but it will usually be possible to get a front door key if you expect to be back late.

Will I be able to keep up activities and outside interests?

People who run residential care homes are usually keen for residents to keep up as many of their previous activities as they can. Sometimes this may mean providing help with transport or someone to accompany you to your destination. This can be arranged in a number of ways, depending on the amount and the kind of help you need. Staff are generally willing to assist if they are able and if they have the time available. Sometimes a volunteer can be recruited to meet the need although homes vary a great deal in the extent to which they have volunteers involved.

Will I be able to keep my pet?

It is unlikely that you will be able to take your pet with you into a residential home. However, some homes may allow small pets, such as budgies, and others may have 'communal' pets, or 'pet visiting' schemes. Such schemes

44

arrange for visits from people with pets for the benefit of residents.

What choice will I have about times and contents of meals?

Some homes will offer residents an early morning cup of tea in bed. Some homes will leave residents to waken in their own time, depending on how flexible mealtimes are. If breakfast is only available at a set time, then staff are likely to waken residents. Some homes will offer tea and toast to residents who wish to have a long lie or who accidentally oversleep! Most homes provide the main meal of the day at lunch-time and offer a high tea, usually something hot, in the late afternoon. In some homes, there is a supper later in the evening which may be provided or laid out for people to help themselves. Hot drinks are usually offered before people go to bed.

Many homes have tea- and coffee-making facilities available for residents to help themselves to as and when they wish. Some homes may even have these facilities in individual bedrooms. Some homes, particularly those run by local authorities and some voluntary agencies, have been designed and built with bedrooms, bathrooms and living-rooms organised in several self-contained units. Residents are accommodated in single bedrooms, usually in units of between eight and 12, although the whole home may accommodate up to 48 people or more. This type of home often has individual kitchens in each unit where residents may prepare meals for themselves, although the main meal is usually centrally prepared and brought to the unit in a heated trolley.

Residents who are able are often encouraged to prepare their own breakfast or high tea, with help from staff if need be. Sometimes baking sessions are organised which can be very popular.

Most homes have central dining-rooms and residents are expected to eat there unless they are ill. Some smaller private homes may not have a dining-room at all and serve all meals to residents in their bedrooms. Homes built on the unit design will probably have sitting/dining-rooms in each unit. Generally, cooks are off-duty at weekends and choice of food may then be more restricted.

Arrangements vary a great deal and you will need to ask individual homes what their arrangements are.

Will there be restrictions on smoking and alcohol?

There are very likely to be some rules about smoking and about the consumption of alcohol. Some homes have bars for their residents and some do not allow alcohol, or are run by religious groups for people who do not drink alcohol. Homes are generally nervous about smoking because of risks associated with fire. If you smoke, you may want to check out what the home's attitude is towards smokers and what facilities it offers them. If you are a non-smoker or a non-drinker it may be important to you to find a home where these activities do not take place. The important thing is for you to find a home which can accommodate your needs.

What access will there be to a telephone?

The telephone can be a lifeline for some people. If you have relatives and friends with whom you can only keep in regular touch by telephone, then this is an aspect of a home that you will regard as very important.

Most homes do now provide a public telephone for the use of residents. However, it is not always possible to have a completely private conversation and it may be in great demand. Increasingly, residents are paying to have their own telephone installed in their room.

Can I get involved in how the home is run?

Local authority social work/services departments believe it is important to offer residents a chance to have some say in how a home is run. Some voluntary and private homes may have a similar belief but it varies a great deal. Some older people do not wish to exercise that kind of influence but some are keen to do so. If you have strong views about residents being able to influence the way support and care is provided in a home you should make this clear to the person who is helping you to choose a home.

Do I have a right to complain if I am dissatisfied?

You have a right to complain, regardless of who is paying your fees. All homes should have a complaints procedure which is clear and easily available to residents. This sort of information should be included in a booklet, if the home has one. In the first instance, dissatisfactions may be best raised with the manager. If they are not satisfactorily dealt with, then the Inspection Unit of the local authority social work/services department can be contacted by you directly or by someone acting on your behalf.

Many people do not find it easy to raise complaints when they have to go on living in a home. They may prefer to keep their dissatisfactions to themselves because they do not want to antagonise staff or they may even fear some kind of retribution if they do complain. However, no home wants or can afford bad publicity and if there is something wrong, this should be raised. A complaint raised by a relative or visitor on your behalf may possibly carry more weight with the organisation running the home.

Some local authorities are establishing 'advocacy schemes' for people living in residential homes. Volunteers either assist the person to make a complaint or make it on their behalf if they are unable to do so themselves.

What happens if I have to go into hospital because of an accident or sudden illness?

If you have a fall and break a bone as a result or have a stroke or other serious illness, your doctor will probably arrange for you to go to hospital, if only for a short while. Whether you will be able to return to the residential care home will depend on what help you will need when you leave hospital, and whether the home feels it can provide this for you.

Residential care homes have to register with local authorities but some homes are also jointly registered as nursing homes with their health authority. They are able to provide a higher level of care should people need it. If you were resident in a jointly registered home you would stand a better chance of being able to return there. This is because all nursing homes have to have qualified nurses on their staff, whereas residential care homes do not.

If you were living in a residential care home and became disabled through accident, illness or just as a result of growing older, the home might suggest that you needed more care and support than they could provide. A move to a nursing home might be suggested. If you were receiving help with your fees from the local authority, the social worker from the social work/ services department would re-assess your needs in consultation with yourself and your relatives. They would then go through the process of advising and offering you a choice of nursing home.

It is becoming less and less likely that you would be offered long term care in an NHS hospital ward unless your medical condition required it. This decision would be taken by the hospital consultant treating you. If the consultant decided that you needed specialist medical or nursing care, you might be placed in a nursing home by the NHS, in which case you would not have to pay the nursing home fees.

What happens when people in residential care homes die there?

Most older people who make a move into some kind of residential care hope that they can stay there for the rest of their lives. It is important to have recorded your wishes with regard to your funeral before you move into a residential care home. This is something you can discuss with your family or with the social worker who is assessing your needs.

Like everything else, the price of funerals continues to rise and is now a considerable sum for people to find.

If the person who would be responsible for arranging the funeral receives a means tested benefit and has a low level of savings, they may be able to get help from the Social Fund in the form of a grant towards funeral costs.

If there is no one prepared or able to meet the cost, the local authority will provide for a simple funeral. Voluntary homes may ask the local authority for help. Private homes will usually refuse to meet the cost and they, too, will turn to the local authority for help.

This chapter has looked at making the decision to move to a residential care home and what living in a residential care home might be like. Many of the questions asked also apply to nursing homes. The following chapter looks at the differences between a nursing home and a residential care home and answers some specific questions about nursing homes.

5

Moving to a Nursing Home

What is the difference between a residential care home and a nursing home?

The main difference is in the level of care which each can provide. Nursing homes must have a qualified nurse as part of their staff and they must also provide facilities which enable them to provide a higher level of care to residents. Residential and nursing homes are registered differently, and have to meet different criteria for registration and inspection.

You may think that a nursing home is only for those who need a very high level of care and this is partly true. However, you may wish to move into a nursing home in order to avoid the risk of maybe having to move from a residential care home to a nursing home if you become very frail or disabled later in life. Like all such decisions there are pros and cons. Sometimes a high proportion of residents of nursing homes have severe memory problems or dementia and people who may be physically frail but still mentally alert may have difficulty finding companionship.

In what circumstances is a nursing home likely to be recommended?

Many people who find themselves in hospital after some sort of crisis in their health may not be able to return home. This may be because they now require a high level of support and care or their home may now be unsuitable for them.

Only older people whose medical condition requires the ongoing treatment or supervision of a consultant geriatrician or psychogeriatrician will be cared for in a long-stay NHS hospital in future. If there are no suitable NHS facilities available, you may be placed in a nursing home.

If your GP decides that you may need to go into hospital for rehabilitation or for treatment of an acute illness or condition, you will still be referred to a Geriatric or Psychogeriatric Assessment Unit or Re-habilitation Unit. If it is an emergency, you may be admitted to the general acute ward of a hospital which has a vacant bed at the time.

Who pays for nursing homes?

Fees for nursing homes are generally higher than those for residential homes, due to the higher level of care involved. Whether you are liable for the nursing home fees depends on whether you are placed there by the local authority or by the NHS. If the medical practitioner in charge of your case decides you need specialist medical care, the fees should be paid for through the NHS. If you are assessed by the local authority as needing nursing home care, the system for getting help with the costs is similar to that for residential homes (see p. 66).

Will I have any choice about which nursing home?

One of the main features of community care is that you should have as much choice as possible over which services you get. If your move is being arranged by the social work/services department, they should try to offer you a choice between several nursing homes whose fees are within the range the local authority is willing to meet. How much choice you are able to exercise will vary. Choice is inevitably restricted by cost, and by what is available.

If you were very keen to move into a nursing home whose fees were above the local authority level but you had a relative or friend who was willing to meet the shortfall, this might be possible. The local authority would probably need some assurance that they would not become liable for the shortfall in the future. In the event that a helping relative or friend could no longer afford to top up your fees, the local authority might ask you to move to a nursing home that was within their price limit.

Can I appeal against a community care assessment?

There is no appeal process, but all local authority social work/service departments must provide a complaints procedure for anyone who disagrees with the assessment or is unhappy about it. You will need to ask for details.

You do have a right to appeal against a decision by a health authority that you no longer need NHS care. You would need to get advice on how to do this.

What points should I consider when choosing a nursing home?

Most of the suggestions made about the important aspects of residential care homes apply if you are

53

contemplating moving into a nursing home (see pp. 33–50).

What sort of accommodation is provided in nursing homes?

It is more common to find shared rooms in nursing homes than in residential care homes; you may find that you have to share a room with more than one person. However, new, purpose-built nursing homes do tend to have single rooms.

What is life inside nursing homes like?

Each nursing home is unique, as is each residential care home. However, it is possible to make a few general points.

You will only have moved into a nursing home if you need nursing care. Depending on the amount of care you need, you will be more or less restricted in making decisions for yourself about your everyday life. You may find the nursing home manages to give people nursing care but still retain a homely atmosphere. Other nursing homes are run on more medical lines and may offer a more hospital-like form of care. For people who have become very frail and need a great deal of nursing care, this can be very reassuring. If you have had a stroke or have broken a leg or have had another serious accident or illness, your self-confidence may have been undermined and it will take time to adjust to your new situation. Caring, competent and confident staff will make this process easier for you.

Will treatment such as physiotherapy and speech therapy be available?

It is impossible to generalise. However, your medical care will continue to be under the supervision of your GP and if the nursing home does not provide such care, your GP can get treatment for you through the NHS, just as if you were in your own home and needing treatment.

Your local authority is responsible for paying for incontinence aids, unless you are paying you own fees, in which case you will be expected to meet the costs yourself.

Where will meals be served?

Larger nursing homes will probably have a central dining room and people who are well enough to eat there will do so. Small nursing homes may not have a dining room as such and meals may be served to residents in their rooms.

Will there be choice offered at mealtimes?

You can find out whether the nursing homes you are considering offer their residents a choice of menus. You may also be interested in the quality and quantity of food offered. If your appetite is less good, it will be particularly important that meals are interesting and nicely presented. If your appetite is as good as ever you will also want to be sure that portions are adequate.

What about visitors?

Each home will differ in its attitude to visitors; you should ask how flexible arrangements are. If residents have single rooms, it is easier to be flexible without infringing the privacy of other residents. However, if bedrooms are shared, visiting times may be restricted.

Will there be staff available at night?

There will certainly be waking staff available over 24 hours to meet residents' needs. Rooms will have call systems so that assistance can be requested when needed.

Will I be able to take in any personal furniture?

This will depend on the size of the accommodation and what you particularly want to take with you. Nursing homes may welcome some of your furniture but some may not have space for it. If you very much want to take some things in with you be sure to enquire about this.

Will my possessions be secure?

It is likely that most nursing homes will offer some lockable drawer or cupboard for you to use. Equally they will not accept liability for loss or theft of precious possessions and the same advice applies about insurance as for residential care homes. You are probably less likely to be offered a key to lock your room but this varies enormously.

Will there be en-suite toilet facilities?

There may be in some homes but they will be the more expensive ones. If you have problems with incontinence or difficulty in getting to the toilet unassisted, you may be offered a commode in your bedroom, particularly for use at night.

Will there be entertainment and outings?

Entertainment may be brought into the home from time to time or staff may take people out for outings. If you don't have relatives or friends who can take you out, there may be a local voluntary group which takes residents out.

Can I complain about the care if I am dissatisfied?

You have a right to complain if a service is unsatisfactory no matter who is paying the fees. The nursing home should provide written information about the complaints procedure – in its brochure or information leaflet, if it has one. It would be best to talk to the manager in the first instance. You, or a relative or friend, can take the matter up with the registration officer at your health authority/board if the matter remains unresolved. Their name, address and telephone number should be part of the information about making complaints provided by the nursing home.

Some health authorities are establishing 'advocacy' schemes for people living in hospitals and nursing homes. Volunteers either assist the person to make a complaint or make it on their behalf if they are unable to do so themselves.

How are nursing homes registered and inspected?

They are registered and inspected by the health authority. However, the local authority social work/ services department may still be responsible for meeting the cost of care, as for residential care homes. Where a home is a jointly registered nursing/residential care home, both authorities will have duties to inspect it. In some areas, social work/services and health personnel have developed standards for care for all registered homes and carry out joint inspections.

Part 3
Income and Finance

Part 3

Income and Finance

Many older people do not claim all the benefits to which they are entitled. You may be entitled to benefits which could help you to manage in your own home. Often people do not realise that there is financial help available to top up their state pension or to help with the costs of disability. This section looks at benefits available to people who live at home as well as people who live in residential or nursing home care.

6

Getting Financial Help

Extra weekly income

If you are on a low income and have savings of less than £8,000 you may be entitled to Income Support. The amount varies, depending on your age and whether you are disabled. If you receive Income Support you may also be entitled to a range of other benefits, including Housing Benefit, Council Tax Benefit, free dental treatment and help with the cost of glasses, and loans and grants from the Social Fund.

Help with rent and Council Tax

Even if you do not qualify for Income Support, you may well be entitled to some Housing Benefit and some Council Tax rebate. If you have savings between £3,000 and £16,000 these will be taken into account when calculating any benefit. If you have more than £16,000 in savings, you will not be eligible.

Help with one-off expenses, e.g. essential household items

If you are on a low income you may be able to claim help from the Benefits Agency to pay for one-off expenses which your weekly income does not cover.

A Community Care Grant or Budgeting Loan can be paid to help you stay in your own home rather than go into residential care. For example, grants or loans can be paid for household items – a cooker, heater, bed and bedding – or minor household repairs.

Extra money if you are disabled or need care

Disability Living Allowance (DLA) is a tax-free benefit for people who need help with personal care or with getting around, or both. This allowance is for people who start to need help when they are under the age of 65. It can be claimed by people between the ages of 65 and 66 so long as their need for help began before their 65th birthday. This allowance does not depend on national insurance contributions and is paid regardless of what your income or savings are. It can mean that you get more Income Support, Housing Benefit and Council Tax rebate.

If you are over 65 and need care, you may be eligible for Attendance Allowance. Like DLA this benefit is paid regardless of income or savings; it is purely related to how much care you need. You must have needed this help for at least six months before claiming any benefit. There are special rules which apply for someone who has a terminal illness to enable them to get this benefit quickly and easily.

Extra money for carers: Invalid Care Allowance

If you are under 65, and are giving at least 35 hours per week regular support to a disabled person, you may be able to claim Invalid Care Allowance. If you qualify you may get more Income Support, Housing Benefit and Council Tax Benefit.

The person being looked after must be getting Disability Living Allowance or Attendance Allowance.

If they live alone, you should get advice before you claim as it may affect their benefit.

How can I claim?

Leaflets about all these benefits and claim forms are available from the Benefits Agency. They can be picked up at your local post office, GP surgery, library or local advice centre or sent to you by post. You can find the telephone number and address of your local Benefits Agency listed in the telephone directory.

You can get help with claiming benefits from a Welfare Benefits Adviser at the local authority social work/service department, or from the Citizens Advice Bureau or local advice centre. Your local Age Concern group may also be able to advise you about who can help you or your relative to complete the forms.

Information on how to claim is now available in a range of languages, so if English is not your first language, do not be put off claiming. If you have a visual impairment the specialist social worker at your local social work/services department should be able to help you complete the application forms.

Age Concern publishes a useful book, *Your Rights* (updated every year) which will tell you about various benefits and how to go about claiming them.

Increasing your weekly income may give you the possibility of acquiring equipment or carrying out alterations to help you remain at home. It may also help you to heat your home better or to pay someone to help you with some of the things you find difficult or impossible to do for yourself.

Raising income from your home

If you own your own home you may wish to realise some of the capital which is tied up in your home. Details of Home Income Plans or annuities which pay the home owner either a lump sum or a regular amount over a fixed period are given in Age Concern's *Factsheet* 12. You should always find out if you are entitled to any benefits first, as any income from an annuity will affect your entitlement to means tested benefits.

7

Paying for Care

Paying for care at home

Each local authority decides what charges it will make for care services which you get at home. They vary as to what income and expenses are taken into account when calculating what, if any, payment you will have to make towards the cost of these services. You should be given information about the charges by the local authority.

Paying for respite care

If a social worker has agreed that you need respite care you may be entitled to help to pay for it.

Local authorities do not all apply the same rules when calculating charges for their services, so be sure to ask for details about charging policies. Some local authorities apply a minimum charge to people having short stays in their residential homes. Others look at your income, and sometimes your savings, to work out how much you should pay.

The charges for home-based schemes may vary, but your local social work/services department will be able to tell you if such a scheme exists in your part of the country and what it costs.

You can arrange and pay for respite care yourself, with a private home or one run by a charitable or voluntary organisation. You can also employ a home care agency to care for you in your own home on a temporary basis, for example to give your carer a holiday. You may find that it does not cost much more to have the care provided in your own home than to stay in a residential or nursing home.

If you have a health need for respite care, the NHS may pay for it.

Paying for residential or nursing home care

What help is available with the cost of care?

To get any financial help with fees for residential or nursing home care from the social work/services department you must be assessed as needing this level of care. If you have capital or savings over £16,000 you will be expected to pay for the full cost of care yourself. You can make your own arrangements to go into a residential or nursing home and pay the fees. However, if in future your savings are going to drop below £16,000 it is worth contacting your local social work/services department before you move to confirm whether they might help meet the cost of fees in the future.

If your savings are below £16,000 you are eligible for help with paying residential or nursing home fees. The amount that the local authority will pay depends on your circumstances and the level of care home fees locally.

How are charges for homes calculated?

The cost of living in a residential care home varies greatly depending on the part of the country in which you are living. Other factors which may affect the cost are the facilities available and the amount of assistance that you need. Weekly charges vary enormously, from under £200 to over £500 a week.

How much will I have to pay?

The amount of help you get depends on your income (this is assessed separately from the income of your husband or wife). You will be expected to contribute nearly all your income towards the costs of care. You are assumed to have a set income from savings between £10,000 and £16,000. Savings below £10,000 are not counted. If you have a private or occupational pension, your spouse (husband or wife), will be able to keep half of it. Certain benefits and income from trusts are not counted. You will only be left with a small amount for personal expenses.

Will my family have to contribute?

The financial assessment for residential and nursing home care is done on the basis of your own income and capital. Your spouse may be expected to make a contribution to the cost of your care. Other family members may contribute to some or all of the costs but they do not have to unless they wish to do so.

The local authority will only pay the fees up to a level it would normally expect to pay for someone with your assessed needs. The local authority may agree to your going into a more expensive home if there is someone else who can make up the difference.

What if I get Attendance Allowance/DLA?

If you are claiming the Disability Living Allowance or the Attendance Allowance when you decide to move into a residential care home, these benefits may be affected. If the social work/services department is helping to meet the cost of your residential care and you were already getting the Attendance Allowance previously, this will stop four weeks after you move into the home. However, if you have made your own arrangements with a private or voluntary home and you were getting the Attendance Allowance or Disability Living Allowance before moving in, these will continue to be paid to you. If you move into a home run by a local authority social work/services department, neither Attendance Allowance nor Disability Living Allowance will continue to be paid to you.

What if I own my own home?

If you own property then the local authority may take its value into account when calculating your financial contribution to your care. It is not taken into account if your spouse or partner, or a relative aged 60 or over or who is disabled still lives in it. The local authority also has discretionary powers to ignore the value of the house in certain other situations. Get advice if you think this might apply to you.

Unless you have enough savings or a sufficiently high income to meet home fees without assistance from the local authority, you will be expected to sell your property in order to release the capital tied up in it. Alternatively, the local authority may draw up a legal agreement with you which guarantees that when the property is finally sold, they will get any money owing to them in connection with supporting you financially in a residential care home.

If you try to dispose of a property or capital before going into a care home in order to avoid having to pay, the local authority may treat you as if you still had the property. If it is passed on to someone else within six months of going into residential care, the charge for the care may be passed on to the person who received the property. If it was longer than six months ago, the local authority has to decide whether you intended to avoid paying for care.

NHS nursing home care

In some cases the health authority may arrange a nursing home place for you under a 'contractual arrangement' – you remain a patient of the NHS and your care will continue to be free of charge although your state pension and benefits will be affected after a time.

What about private insurance schemes?

Insurance schemes are available which are designed to help you pay for either care at home or in a care home, should the need arise. You should contact individual insurance companies to compare different policies and you should note any exclusion clauses which might limit your cover in the future. Costs vary a great deal and premiums may be very expensive. With some types of policy it takes time for your money to grow, so policies are best taken out in middle age. Payments from certain types of long-term care insurance are exempt from tax: individual companies offering such products should be able to advise you whether the benefit paid out would be exempt from tax.

It is advisable to find out what financial help might be available from other sources before you commit yourself to a particular policy.

Conclusion

The whole area of community care is still changing and developing. Until relatively recently, long stay care tended to be provided in hospital. The emphasis now is to support older people and enable them to remain in their own homes where possible. Health authorities/ boards and social work/services departments are expanding and developing community-based services to make this possible. New ways of meeting needs imaginatively and sensitively are being tried out all over the country, often on a trial or 'pilot' basis in the first instance. You may be lucky enough to have such schemes in your area and be able to benefit from them.

One important result of the community care changes is that the voice of the consumer of services – the older person and any family member or friend who provides them with a great deal of support (often referred to as the carer) is now supposed to be heard. Of course, making this intention into a reality is not always easy, which is why advocacy schemes are coming into existence. These schemes recruit volunteers to assist or represent the service user in articulating their needs and wishes and in making complaints to the relevant authority.

It is impossible to cover every aspect of care and support in old age because, as you will have realised by now, it is a complicated issue. Because every older person is unique, one person's preference might be quite unacceptable or unsuitable for another. What this book has tried to do is to give you a flavour of the kinds of choices which may be available to you so that, if you wish to remain in your own home, you can get the help you need. On the other hand, if you want to go into residential care or a nursing home, you are now only able to exercise that choice for yourself if you can pay the cost of it entirely out of your own resources. If you need, or are likely to need financial help from the local authority to meet the cost, then a social worker will assess whether that is the best solution.

This book should help you to make at least some informed choices about how you (or the person you are helping to make these important decisions) are supported or cared for when the need arises.

Useful Addresses

Age Concern Cymru
   4th Floor, 1 Catherdral Road, Cardiff CF1 9SD
   Tel.: 01222 371566

Age Concern England
   Astral House, 1268 London Road, London SW16 4ER
   Tel.: 0181 679 8000

Age Concern Northern Ireland
   3 Lower Crescent, Belfast BT7 1NR
   Tel.: 01232 245729

Age Concern Scotland
   113 Rose Street, Edinburgh EH2 3DT
   Tel.: 0131 220 3345

*Alzheimer's Disease Society (**England**)*
   Gordon Terrace, 10 Greencoat Place, London SW1P 1PH
   Tel.: 0171 306 0606

Alzheimer's Disease Society Wales
   Tonna Hospital, Neath, SA11 3LX
   Tel.: 01639 641938

Alzheimer's Scotland: Action on Dementia
   8 Hill Street, Edinburgh EH1 1TB
   Tel.: 0131 225 1453
   The three Alzheimer's associations listed above support
   people with dementia and their families and carers. They also
   provide information about all forms of dementia and run
   local groups for patients and their relatives.

Arthritis Care
   18 Stephenson Way, London NW1 2HD
   Tel.: 0171 916 1500 *or* freephone Helpline 0800 289 170.
   Advice and information from trained counsellors. Local
   branches for people with arthritis and their families.

British Federation of Care Home Proprietors
852 Melton Road, Thurmaston, Leicester LE4 8BN
Tel.: 0116 640095.
Standards of care in all homes are independently monitored
in accordance with national guidelines. The federation can
provide lists of members in all areas.

British Diabetic Association
10 Queen Anne Street, London W1M 0BD
Tel.: 0171 323 1531.
Help for all diabetics and their families.

Parkinson's Disease Society
22 Upper Woburn Place, London WC1H 0RA.
Tel.: 0171 383 3513. Helpline 0171 388 5798

British Red Cross Society
9 Grosvenor Crescent, London SW1X 7EJ.
Tel.: 0171 235 5454.
Services mainly provided by volunteers and available from
local centres: home nursing, equipment loan, transport,
holidays, domiciliary and respite care.

Carers National Association
20-25 Glasshouse Yard, London EC1A 4JS
Tel.: 0171 490 8818

Carers National Association Scotland
162 Buchanan Street, 3rd floor, Glasgow G1 2LL
Tel.: 0141 333 9495

Carers National Association in Wales
Pantglas Industrial Estate, Bedwas, Newport, South Wales
NP1 8DR
Tel.: 01222 880176
The three national carers associations listed above are
campaigning and information-giving organisations which
seek to promote the interests of all people who are 'carers'.
This includes those who are looking after someone who has a
physical or mental disability – of any age. They have
branches all over the country.

Carematch

c/o Leonard Cheshire Foundation, 26 – 29 Maunsel Street, London SW10 2QN

Tel.: 0171 828 1822

A service mainly for physically disabled people seeking residential or nursing home care. Details of homes throughout the country.

Caresearch

ARC House, Marsden Street, Chesterfield, S40 1JT

Tel.: 01246 555043

Information about homes across the UK for people with learning disabilities of all ages.

Charity Search

25 Portview Road, Avonmouth, Bristol BS11 9LD

Tel.: 0117 982 4060.

A charity providing free advice for older people, linking them with established charities which may be able to help with funds for extra costs at home or for shortfalls in fees for residential and nursing homes.

The Continence Foundation

2 Doughty Street, London WC1N 2PH

Can provide advice and information in response to enquiries by letter or the *Continence Helpline* (Tel.: 0191 213 0050) gives telephone advice to those affected by incontinence and their families.

Counsel and Care

Twyman House, 16 Bonny Street, London NW1 9PG

Tel.: 0171 485 1566

A charity which provides advice for older people, their families and professionals on charges, benefits, community care and available charitable grants.

Crossroads (Association of Crossroads Care Attendant Schemes)

10 Regent Place, Rugby, Warwickshire CV21 2PN

Tel.: 01788 573 653

Schemes across the UK which aim to relieve carers by providing care for a person in their own home.

Disabled Living Centres Council

Winchester House, 11 Cranmer Road, London SW9 6EJ

Tel.: 0171 266 2059

Information about Disabled Living Centres in the UK.

Elderly Accommodation Counsel
46A Chiswick High Road, London W4 1SZ
Tel.: 181 995 8320 or 0181 742 1182
A registered charity which maintains a national database of
all forms of private and voluntary accommodation for older
people – sheltered housing, residential care, nursing homes
and hospices. EAC can provide you with a list of homes,
within a certain price range, in the area of your choice and
also give advice on possible sources of top-up funding for
those needing help with care home fees.

Energy Advice Centres
For advice on energy efficiency and cutting bills contact your
local Energy Advice Centre. For information on grants
available for insulation and draught-proofing contact the
Energy Action Grants Association on freephone 0800 181 667 *or*
write to EAGA Ltd, Freepost, PO Box 130, Newcastle upon
Tyne NE99 2RP.

National Care Homes Association
5 Bloomsbury Place, London WC1A 2QA
Tel.: 0171 436 1871

Royal Association for Disability and Rehabilitation (RADAR)
12 City Forum, 250 City Road, London EC1V 8AF
Tel.: 0171 250 3222. Minicom: 0171 250 4119

Disability Scotland
Princes House, 5 Shandwick Place, Edinburgh EH2 4RG
Tel.: 0131 229 8632

Disability Wales
Llys Ifor, Crescent Road, Caerphilly CF83 1XL
Tel.: 01222 887325
The three national disability associations above give
information and advice on access, aids and adaptations,
housing, holidays, mobility, education, employment and
social services.

Registered Nursing Homes Association
Calthorpe House, Hagley Road, Edgbaston, Birmingham B16
8QY
Tel.: 0121 454 2511
Provides information on registered nursing homes in the UK

and the Republic of Ireland which conform to certain standards and which have been visited by the Association.

The Relatives Association
5 Tavistock Place, London WC1H 9SS
Tel.: 0171 916 6055
Gives advice and help to relatives and friends about the care of older people in homes. The association is committed to improving the standards of residential care through the active involvement of relatives. They aim to promote a common understanding between relatives, residents, home providers and staff.

Royal National Institute for the Blind (RNIB
224 Great Portland Street, London W1N 6AA.
Tel.: 0171 3388 1266
Provides advice and services for people with a visual handicap.

Royal National Institute for the Deaf (RNID)
19–23 Featherstone Street, London EC1 8SL
Tel.: 0171 296 800
Provides advice and services for people with a hearing impairment.

Racial Equality Councils
For advice for people from minority ethnic groups. Look in the phone book for your local council.

Stroke Association
CHSA House, Whitecross Street, London EC1Y 8JJ
Tel.: 0171 490 7999
Helps stroke sufferers and their families with advice on rehabilitation. Lists available of local groups.

United Kingdom Home Care Association
42 Barnstead Road, Carshalton Beeches, Surrey SM5 3NW.
Tel.: 01422 832559
An association of providers of care at home, with a code of practice for members. Lists of members available.

Women's Royal Voluntary Sevice (WRVS)
Milton Hill Training Centre, Milton Hill Abingdon, Oxford OX13 6AF.

Tel.: 01235 442 900
Local WRVS branches provide services and support,
including in many areas meals on wheels. Over 125,000
volunteers (both men and women) work throughout Britian.

Further Reading

Alzheimer Scotland Action on Dementia. *A positive choice: choosing long-stay care for a person with dementia.* Edinburgh: Alzheimer Scotland Action on Dementia (ASAAD), 1996.

Alzheimer Scotland Action on Dementia. *Dementia: money and legal matters, a guide for carers.* Edinburgh: Alzheimer Scotland Action on Dementia (ASAAD), 1996.

Age Concern England; National Housing and Town Planning Council. *A buyer's guide to retirement housing.* London: Age Concern England (ACE), 1995.

Age Concern Factsheet* 6. *Finding help at home.*

Age Concern Factsheet* 8. *Rented accommodation for older people.*

Age Concern Factsheet* 8a. *Very sheltered housing.* (Available in Scotland only.)

Age Concern Factsheet* 10. *Local authority charging procedures for residential and nursing home care.*

Age Concern Factsheet* 11. *Preserved entitlement to income support.* (For people living in private or voluntary homes on or before 31 March 1993.)

Age Concern Factsheet* 12. *Raising an income or capital from your home.*

Age Concern Factsheet* 13. *Older home owners – financial help with repairs.*

Age Concern Factsheet* 18. *A brief guide to money benefits.*

Age Concern Factsheet* 23. *Help with continence.*

Age Concern Factsheet* 24. *Buying a house when older.*

Age Concern Factsheet* 29. *Finding residential and nursing home accommodation.*

Age Concern Factsheet* 32. *Disability and ageing: your rights to social services.*

Age Concern Factsheet* 34. *Attendance allowance.*

Age Concern Factsheet* 38. *Treatment of the former home as capital for people in residential and nursing homes.*

Age Concern Factsheet* 39. *Paying for care in a residential or nursing home if you have a partner.*

Age Concern Factsheet* 40. *Transfer of assets and paying for care in a residential or nursing home.*

Brown, Paul; Mountfield, Anne; Patel, Alka. *Pensioners and carers: help for older people in need and advice for their carers.* London: Directory of Social change, 1995.

Counsel and Care. *From home to a home: a study of older people's hopes, expectations and experiences of residential care.* London: Counsel and Care, 1992.

Department of Health. *Moving into a care home: things you need to know.* Department of Health, 1996.

Hinton, Cecil. *Using your home as capital: a guide to raising cash from the value of your home.* London: Age Concern England (ACE), (updated annually).

Lay, Chris; Woods, Bob. *Caring for the person with dementia: a guide for families and other carers.* 4th edition. London: Alzheimer's Disease Society.

Lewycka, Marina. *Choices for the carer of an elderly relative.* Series: Caring in a Crisis.** London: Age Concern England (ACE), 1995.

Lewycka, Marina. *Finding and paying for residential and nursing home care.* Series: Caring in a Crisis.** London: Age Concern England (ACE), 1994.

Lewycka, Marina. *What to do and who to turn to.* Series: Caring in a Crisis.** London: Age Concern England (ACE), 1993.

McKay, Colin; Patrick, Hilary. *The care maze: the law and your rights to community care in Scotland.* (Applies only to Scotland.) Glasgow: ENABLE/Scottish Association for Mental Health, 1995.

Meridith, Barbara. *The community care handbook.* (Applies only in England and Wales.) London: Age Concern England (ACE), 1995.

Thompson, Keith. *Caring for an elderly relative: a guide to home care.* New edition. London: Optima, 1993.

West, Sally. *Your rights: a guide to money benefits for older people.* London: Age Concern England (ACE), (updated annually).

White, Sheila. *Going home from hospital.* Series: Caring in a Crisis.** London: Age Concern England (ACE), 1994.

Footnotes

* Factsheets are available free, up to a maximum of five copies, from the appropriate national Age Concern organisation (see list of useful addresses, pp. 73–77). Please send a large stamped addressed envelope. Factsheets are revised and updated as necessary. For information on subscribing to all the Age Concern Factsheets please contact Age Concern England.

** The series *Caring in a Crisis* has been written for older people and their families and friends, to guide them through the key stages of a crisis and helps you make practical, informed decisions.

Index

The Stationery
Office

Published by The Stationery Office and available from:

The Stationery Office Bookshops
71 Lothian Road, Edinburgh EH3 9AZ
(counter service only)
0131-479 3141 Fax 0131-479 3142
49 High Holborn, London WC1V 6HB
(counter service and fax orders only)
Fax 0171-831 1326
68-69 Bull Street, Birmingham B4 6AD
0121-236 9696 Fax 0121-236 9699
33 Wine Street, Bristol BS1 2BQ
0117-926 4306 Fax 0117-929 4515
9-21 Princess Street, Manchester M60 8AS
0161-834 7201 Fax 0161-833 0634
16 Arthur Street, Belfast BT1 4GD
01232 238451 Fax 01232 235401
The Stationery Office Oriel Bookshop
The Friary, Cardiff CF1 4AA
01222 395548 Fax 01222 384347

The Stationery Office publications are also available from:
The Publications Centre
(mail, telephone and fax orders only)
PO Box 276, London SW8 5DT
General enquiries 0171-873 0011
Telephone orders 0171-873 9090
Fax orders 0171-873 8200

Accredited Agents
(see Yellow Pages)
and through good booksellers

Printed in Scotland for The Sationery Office Limited by CC No. 3093 15C 6/97

Cupcake Mystery

HELLO KITTY ADVENTURE·

To rene

Y

The at